PROPERTY DE` BEGINNERS

A BEGINNERS GUIDE TO PROPERTY DEVELOPMENT

By Steve Chandler

Legal Disclaimer

To every person who loves property development and wants to learn more.

Acknowledgements

I wish to thank the numerous people that I have worked with over the past three decades; you have been my inspiration for creating this book.

CONTENTS

Introduction

What an amazing and financially rewarding career property development can provide. If that's what you want to achieve and you are just beginning, this book is for you.

Let me start by saying this: I love property development!

For over thirty years I have been part of the property development industry. I have been associated with a wide variety of property development projects including public infrastructure assets (bridges, libraries, railway interchanges, ferry wharves), apartments, clubs, schools, shopping centres, condominiums, warehouses, manufacturing and production facilities, heritage building refurbishments, food courts, land subdivisions, cold stores, shipping container terminals, demolition and remediation projects; and the list goes on.

Over the past fifteen years I have also had a substantial exposure to property development related litigation and disputes.

I am the CEO of *LEFTA Corporation Pty Limited* ('LEFTA®"), a property development strategy, advisory and consultancy firm that assists people with their property development projects and also assists in the resolution of disputes which occur occasionally.

Since 2006 LEFTA® has assisted numerous clients with their projects and now I have chosen to expand this assistance via literature.

We all live in a property that was developed by someone at some time in the past and in the majority of cases it was developed for profit.

Similarly we all work in a property that was developed by someone at some time in the past and most likely for profit also.

Everywhere we look and everywhere we go we find property; and as our population continues to grow there is demand for infrastructure (roads, bridges, tunnels, water, sewerage, gas, electricity etc.), employment generating industry (office buildings, warehouses, manufacturing facilities, laboratories etc.) and somewhere for the population to live (housing, apartments and condominiums etc.). Everything is property related.

There is opportunity everywhere to develop property for profit.

All you have to do is find the opportunity and create the profit!

Some might say that finding the appropriate site is the hardest part of property development, and they are correct, to a certain extent. But after you find a site you have to acquire it and then manage a long term project through uncertain economic conditions.

If you remember the global financial crisis ("GFC") of 2008 then you will understand what I mean by uncertain economic conditions. If you do not recall the GFC then you may wish to read a little about the financial meltdown that occurred all over the world which virtually nobody saw coming. Those who did were very fortunate.

As a property developer you must de-risk your project as much as possible at every stage of the process. Property development simply put is a process, just like baking a cake.
First you have to find a site, ensure it is appropriate to develop and then acquire it.

Once the property is acquired you are only partially committed to its development; you could choose to divest the property at certain times.

But if you proceed you must create an appropriately designed building for the appropriate price within an appropriate timeframe, obtaining the appropriate authority approvals, and divest the end product at the appropriate time.

This is just a process that needs to be managed. However like any new cook just having the ingredients in front of you doesn't automatically assure you of success.

In my experience not all property development projects are profitable; errors are made and economic conditions change. You must be appropriately prepared in case this happens to you.

Don't let this last statement put you off property development. You need to be aware that negative things can happen and that you must have an appropriate strategy in place to deal with things as they occur. There is no benefit in crying if something happens, you have to take action to sort out the issue, and fast!

Property development can be very rewarding both personally and financially if you appropriately prepare yourself.

My disclaimer to you is this; this book has been written to inform you of my knowledge and experiences in property development, it is not advice and does not include every matter that should be considered when undertaking a property development project. It is a guide to the types of issues that may be appropriate to consider on a property development project. It is essential to the successful outcome of your project that you obtain expert advice throughout your project.

I'm certain you will find the following chapters useful to you as you prepare your journey into property development.

One quick note before I move on; if you have already completed a property development project of your own, this book may not be for you as you will already have experienced some or most of what this book contains.

For everyone else, let's get stuck into the property development process.

Why develop property for profit?

Why not? Really; why not? Why can't you develop property for profit?

There is no reason why you or anyone can't develop property for profit. All you have to do is know how!

OK, I admit that's a big one! But once you know how is there anything stopping you? I mean once you know what you need to do you can do it; right?

Of course you can. And that's why you are reading this book.

So let's answer the question in the name of this chapter; why develop property for profit?

I believe the answer is simple, because you wouldn't take the risk doing it if there wasn't a profit in it. That was simple!

It's simply risk and reward in action. Whenever you take a risk doing something you have an expectation of being rewarded in some manner.

For example, people who do extreme sports, that we "normal" people may consider risky, do so for an expectation of getting an adrenalin rush (or some similar reward). Some may even be paid handsomely to do these sports by sponsors who want to advertise their products. Whatever their motivator is, this is their reward.

What motivates you?

Do you love money? Do you love the lifestyle that money can provide? Whatever it is, if it is strong enough and you love property then property development may be the right medium for you to earn profit or build upon your asset base.

Profit is a reward for taking a risk. The secret is to minimise your risk and maximise your profit.

Learning: Reward is relative to the risk required to achieve it. The secret is to minimise your risk whilst retaining the reward.

Risk

Property development is full of risk. I recommend that you seek appropriate legal, professional and financial advice prior to and throughout your project. Why do I recommend this? I recommend this as it is the prudent thing to do. Experienced property developers obtain advice prior to and throughout their projects and so should you.

The word "risk" strikes fear into the hearts of many people more than any other I know. Are you risk averse? If you are then my experience tells me that you are suitable for property development; if you are willing to take risks then property development may not be appropriate for you.

Does this confuse you?

Some people think that property development is high risk. In my experience property developers are very risk averse; they attempt to mitigate risk wherever possible.

Property developers prepare detailed risk assessment practices to reduce the potential for anything to go wrong on their projects, particularly as projects usually take a substantial period of time from when a site is acquired until it is completed.

Before you even consider acquiring a site you need to understand the risk associated with your proposed property development.

In my experience it is important to know what your opportunity is. You must know what problem you are going to solve by developing your project.

For example, is there a shortage of housing in the area that you wish to develop in? Or maybe there is insufficient retail space in the neighbourhood as people have to drive miles to get to the shops. Perhaps there isn't enough employment in the area and you believe that there needs to be more commercial space available. Whatever the driver is for you to develop, you must know this in detail.

Do your market research. Have an independent expert review your research and provide you with their opinion. Remember, you may be intending to spend (and potentially make) millions of dollars on a project, you don't want to risk this on poor research, do you?

One of my past clients did their own research for their project and ended up suffering a major loss. I clawed back some money but couldn't save the project.

Once you know and understand your driver for your property development project you have removed your first risk.

As with any good property developer, create a risk matrix of items that could negatively affect your project. Once you have this list you can start to rate what the likelihood is for these things occurring and what the potential outcome of such events would be on your project.

When you have all this information collated into a single document you can see where your major risks are and where risks relate to each other. Now you can start to prepare mitigative strategies, or methods by which you will reduce the risk to an acceptable level for you.

You may not be able to mitigate every risk to an acceptable level and you will need to be cognisant of this. If this occurs consider whether there is any alternative method available to you or if you can eliminate this item completely? If you can't then perhaps the current development proposal is not suitable to undertake.

Starting a project that has an unmitigated major risk with high probability of occurring is not what I would call wise. This one issue could cost you all the profit on your project or worse!

The GFC hurt a lot of property developers however, with hindsight I can say that one risk that could have been identified is a major shift in the market.

What this means is that property developers could have identified a risk of the market turning at some point during their project, particularly given the continuous growth that occurred for a number of years preceding the GFC.

As a property developer you must always consider macro-economic issues in your risk assessment. Even though it has been a number of years since the GFC it remains valid to consider the global economic conditions and the cost of funds when undertaking projects. This simply means that you must structure your projects to keep yourself distanced from any financial fallout if things don't go your way.

Throughout the remainder of this book I will identify a number of risks that you may wish to consider. As I do not know what your intended project is or what it might be I cannot provide specific information for you. However the issues I will discuss are typical of some property development projects.

Learning: Risk identification and mitigation will make (or save) you a lot of money.

Joint venture partners

One option for beginners is to form a joint venture. This means finding someone (or a company) to undertake the project with you. This is an easy way to reduce your risk, if you find the right joint venture partner.

Property development projects are like playing a game; it's always better to have someone on your team that knows how to play. So if you choose to do a joint venture, make sure you find a partner that has experience. You will learn a lot from them and they will also learn from you, yes, from you too! Even though you are a beginner you will bring your own knowledge and experience to the joint venture that your partner doesn't have and, being a novice, you will be asking a lot of valid questions, which will benefit you both.

Joint ventures can take many forms. You could partner with a property owner that wants to develop their land, partner with someone that has done a couple of very small property developments and wants a partner to do something a bit larger, partner with someone with equity that wants to invest into a property development, or you could partner with someone that wants a finished product for themselves.

Joint venture partners exist in these and many other forms. If you are serious about property development then you need to talk to people about it to "sound them out" on whether they are interested also.

If you partner with a property owner they may only wish to provide the land into the joint venture and you provide the remainder of the expertise and funding. Keep in mind that financiers are almost certain to require security over the existing land before advancing construction funding. This issue and various others must be addressed in the partnering agreement.

Where you partner with someone on a 50/50 basis you may wish to consider whether one of the partners is going to be able to draw a monthly fee for management of the project (this can be called a "project management fee").

If your partner is an equity investor only then consider how you will repay this equity and what this equity will actually cost you. Will it be a percentage of profit or will it be a loan? Or does the equity investor wish to inject equity into your company and have a shareholding? Make sure you understand what an equity investor requires and how this will affect you both now and in the future. If you sell some of your shares you are selling future company profits, not just the current project profits.

You can use any terminology that you like to describe joint venture arrangements (for example you could use the term "development agreement") so long as the agreement between the partners is in writing and clearly identifies the agreed terms of the partnering.

Whenever you intend to undertake any type of partnering arrangement make sure you obtain legal advice on the structure and the risk that each partner carries.

Learning: Joint venturing is a good way to reduce risk, improve expertise and potentially generate larger profits.

Feasibility

Before you commit any money into a property development project you need to know if it is likely to be profitable!

To do this you will need to undertake some sort of analysis which can be called a feasibility study. This will entail best and worst case scenarios and sensitivity analysis if something goes wrong.

Feasibility studies can be created in many forms however I have used two basic formats in my career; these are a static feasibility and a cashflow. I call them both by the generic names "feasibility" and "feaso".

A static feasibility is a one page document that includes the major headline items that will incur cost or generate revenue for the project. Some examples of these headline items are listed below.

A cashflow includes the major headline items and the minor items associated with the headline ones and then projects a cost for each of these over a period of time so that every month you can see what your projected cashflow position will be.

At the very early stages of a project you might only do a static feasibility to see how the project financial outcomes look. If financial outcomes work for you then you may do a cashflow feasibility to verify your thoughts and assumptions. Keep in mind that your feasibility will always change as you discover more and more information pertaining to the site and the market conditions.

Hopefully you will have the market conditions researched as part of your due diligence so only the site can surprise you. This is where due diligence is essential, which is discussed in a latter chapter.

So how or what should be included in a feasibility? That depends on your project however the following list of headline items will assist you.

- Purchase price of site
- Closing costs for purchase
- Any acquisition costs (legal, taxes, authority fees and charges)
- Holding costs for the site until completion
- Financier fees and charges
- Interest
- Design
- Remediation
- Construction
- Insurance
- Authority contributions
- Sales and marketing
- Real Estate Agent fees
- Consultants
- Taxes
- Contingency value (percentage of total costs)
- Gross realisation

As you start to consider these items you will realise that there are many more that will apply to your project and each of these items have other minor items that are incorporated into them. You need to consider these major and minor items and any other items that are applicable to your project.

Now start applying costs to each of these items.

Don't just guess these costs, research what they will be or what they are likely to be but again seek advice and factor in contingencies that may impact on the final outcome.

Talk to builders, consultants and authorities. Remember that when you discuss these things the answer you get will be varied as you do not have any specific project documents for people to respond to.

What you are likely to find is that as you work your way through your list you will have more poignant questions for the people you have already spoken with. Wait until you work your way through the entire list before calling the first person again; you will have a lot more information to discuss with them the second time around.

Now you have a feasibility study completed with a bottom line. If the bottom line isn't enough then don't do it! If it is enough for you to proceed then you need to acquire a site but again, make sure you seek appropriate advice before signing a contract.

Learning: Talk to the experts to obtain the input information for your feasibility. The more accurate your feasibility the more likely you will be to make a profit.

Site selection

Let's assume that you haven't joint ventured with a property owner, that you have created an indicative feasibility analysis that is positive and now you have to locate a site. How do you do this?

Firstly, you must know what your target market is for your proposed development. For now let's simply say you are going to develop apartments as there is a demand for medium density housing in the locality you wish to develop in.

So now you know that you must have a site that will allow medium density housing to be developed upon it.

Your local authority will have a town or urban plan (or similar) that clearly dictates where particular types of development can occur. There will be a zone that permits medium density housing; find this zone and look at the town plan map of your target area to see where you must concentrate your search.

The town plan map will show you the zone, usually in a particular colour, overlaid onto a street map type of document. These can be hard copy documents or accessible via the internet. These days the internet accessible documents are standard however you can still visit your local authority and look at their large scale zoning maps and talk to one of their town planners to get some insight.

Now you have some guidance on where you can develop, it still isn't time to go knocking on doors to find a property. The area covered by the zoning overlay is massive (usually) and includes a substantial number of properties that you could never visit in a reasonable amount of time.

You need to refine your search area substantially.

To do this, think of what will assist you to sell your apartments. What would a buyer want close to their new home or investment property?; public transport?; shops?; restaurants?; employment opportunities (i.e. factories and offices)?; parks?; child care centres?; universities?; any other infrastructure? What would anyone want to be close to? Or, what would people not want to be near?

Use these or any other things that you deem appropriate to give yourself some guidance on where to start your search.

If you can locate an area that has all the relevant and appropriate attributes and you can find a site in this area, you have just de-risked part of your project. You would have a development with all the right drawcards to attract people to the location.

With your refined search area now established its time to look for appropriate sites.

So what are you looking for? What does the appropriate site need to have to be of interest to you? What are your minimum requirements?

Your static feasibility model will be able to provide you with guidance on what minimum size parcel of land you need to generate the potential profit you desire.

Armed with the list of items you need to achieve for a site to be appropriate for development you can start researching suitable sites on the town plan map. There is no need to go knocking on doors just yet.

Search the town plan map conscientiously and in a matter of time you may locate a few potentially appropriate sites. Of course you will not be able to check off every requirement on your list of items but you will be able to confirm a few of them. If you can't confirm a few of them then the sites are not appropriate.

Now you have narrowed down your search area to some specific sites.

I love the internet! I can research potential development sites to my heart's content using the internet. Use the internet and take an aerial view of the site. You can also look at the site from street level. The images may not be up to date but they will show you a lot of information that should be able to tick some more boxes on your items list.

If the sites you look at tick some more boxes for you then it's time to research ownership details and prices in the area. You can do this on the internet also.

A very important piece of information is property ownership details. This tells you what type of entity owns the property (is it a person, a company, a charity, a church, or government). This will provide guidance on how to approach the owner for your potential negotiations.

You may also find out what price they paid for the property and when they purchased it.

Let's assume that you have undertaken all your due diligence necessary to acquire a site and you're now ready to make your move and acquire the property. You've done your feasibility and you know how much you can afford to pay for the site to make your profit.

Time to acquire that site!

Learning: You must know what your target market needs and wants so that you can give them a project that ticks all the right boxes for them.

Due diligence

It never ceases to amaze me how much effort people put into finding a new stereo, computer or car yet don't do the same for a new home or investment property.

When you look at the time/effort compared to the value of the product being sought, any piece of property that is likely to end up with you having a long term liability and an opportunity to realise capital gain has got to be worth doing substantial research *before* proceeding.

When it comes to property development, the amount of research required is substantially more than what you would do for your home or an investment property. Remember that you are planning a project that might take two or three years to complete from the time you acquire the site. A lot can happen in this time.

There are also other factors that you must consider that relate to risk management. That's right, risk management starts even before you acquire a property.

So what type of due diligence do you need to do before you acquire a site?

Let's consider this for a moment. Again let's assume you are intending to build medium density housing.

You must know what your market requires; what is the market demand? What is the market price for the product the market requires? This is the essential first step. Identify a market and its price point.

Once you identify a market you can propose a development.

The next thing you need to do is determine if the proposed development is permissible where the site is, which comes from the town plan map. Then you need to determine what town planning constraints and attributes are relevant to the site, which comes from the town planning legislation and development controls.

You need to have undertaken a preliminary feasibility to determine whether these attributes and constraints are appropriate for your project to be profitable.

What has the site been used for in the past? Was it a chemical factory or an abattoir? Whatever the former use of the site has been you need to know so that you can determine whether there is likely to be any contamination present.

Regardless of whether you are able to sign a purchase agreement where the vendor takes all liability for contamination on the site, in my experience you are likely to become delayed due to unforeseen circumstances. Contamination in the ground and in the groundwater cannot be readily determined even with substantial testing.

What this means is that your project is likely to be delayed when it comes time to remediate the site, whether this is done by removal or on-site treatment. Unforseen delays cost you time and in some cases potential litigation. Time costs you money. Money reduces your contingency. Reduced contingency increases your risk.

What or who are your neighbours? Are they housing or commercial properties? Are you going to develop the first medium density property in the neighbourhood? What impact may your proposed development have on the local community?

If you are proposing something new and different to the current streetscape you might find you will have some local opposition. Find out about the local community action groups that may object. When you know about them you can strategize.

Are there any issues associated with the existing property on the site? Remember that you are going to be the owner of this property until it is demolished to make way for your development. Are there any issues that will cost you money such as maintenance costs?

Consider that you may not commence your development for a year or two, or even longer if the market changes and you shelve your proposed development. You are buying an existing asset, you need to know everything about the property you possibly can and whether it can still provide you with a reasonable cashflow in the meantime.

Is it riddled with asbestos, polychlorinated biphenyls (PCB's) or other hazardous materials? These can cost you a substantial amount of money to remove or to make safe. You must be aware of these types of issues.

If you are acquiring an existing property, what tenancy agreements exist and what are the terms of occupancy? If you need to terminate a lease or leases to start your development, can you? What are the tenancy issues applicable to the site?

Are there any easements or rights of carriageway, support, access and the like over the proposed site? Does any public infrastructure travel over, through or under the site? If so, can you relocate these or remove them?

Due diligence is a very detailed assessment of all the potential attributes and constraints associated with a property.

Any property that is your proposed development site has issues that require investigation, you may wish to investigate as many of these issues as possible before you approach the owner and start to negotiate. Forewarned is forearmed as they say.

Once you have offer and acceptance based upon then known information you are likely to require an exclusive due diligence period where you can carry out physical investigations to confirm what you already know (or suspect) and to determine if there is anything else that you don't know.

You will need to engage relevant experts at this stage.

Don't forget to update your feasibility study with any new information you discover. Are you still making the required profit?

With this new information you may wish to renegotiate the purchase price and/or terms.

Due diligence is an essential component of being a profitable property developer.

Learning: De-risking your project from before you acquire a property is good business practice; due diligence does this.

Acquisition

You've done some high level due diligence on appropriate locations to develop. You've also spoken to a number of people about the likely costs of development and have created a feasibility study that provides you with the base knowledge and assumptions necessary to acquire a site including best and worst case scenarios.

Your research into potential sites has indicated a number of properties of interest and you have further researched these on the internet, resulting in a short list of potential properties.

You have now undertaken off-site due diligence on each of these potential properties and you have further reduced your short list of potential properties to a handful of what you believe are the best possible properties for your proposed development.

At this stage I would be ranking the sites by preference. Number one being the best site, number two being the next best and so forth.

So how are you going to acquire the number one site? How are you going to approach and convince the owner to sell to you?

This is one of the hardest questions to answer. Some people are born negotiators, some learn the art, and others really struggle with the whole concept.

Your options as I see them are to either approach the owner yourself or utilise the services of an agent to act on your behalf.

One thing I know for sure, it's negotiation time! Let's assume you are going to approach the owner yourself.

Negotiation is a very personal matter. I'm not going to even try to tell you how to negotiate but I will tell you a couple of things you may wish to consider before you start your negotiations.

If the site is absolutely amazing and has everything going for it to make a profit, then you don't want to lose it; right? Consider the "what if" scenarios that may occur when you approach the owner.

What if the owner doesn't want to sell to a property developer who will make a "huge profit" whilst they only get a market price?

What if they want to be part of the development as a joint venture partner?

What if they don't want to sell now but may want to do so in the future?

You need to have an answer to all of these scenarios and more. Be prepared for a joint venture arrangement. Be willing to offer to purchase the site under option to settle in the future (this secures the property now and gives you the right to acquire the property in the future at an agreed price). Be willing to pay an above market price if it is feasible to do so.

There is one essential component of acquiring a site that I believe cannot be overlooked, it's securing the site now without paying for it. You don't want to pay for a site until you are, at least, ready to start construction.

Purchasing the site under option (as mentioned above) is one way that this can occur. Imagine having the right to purchase the property at some time in the future at an agreed price but not having to pay for it now. Property options are one method of acquiring property now but paying later.

The joint venture approach is similar. But with a joint venture you can negotiate so that the property owner has to wait until all the revenues from the finished product have been collected and that the financier has been paid out *before* paying them anything!

When acquiring a site remember that you want to be able to create your development design, obtain authority approvals and tender your building work before you pay for the site, at a minimum!

Learning: Do a static feasibility on your preferred site before talking to the owner. You will need to know how much you can afford to offer them for the site so you can have meaningful dialogue with them.

Legal advice

I'm not a lawyer and this book is not legal advice. But I will give you this advice; seek legal advice before you do anything.

The legal world surrounding property development is fraught with danger for newcomers.

There are all sorts of legal matters that will require appropriate advice such as site acquisition and conveyance, joint venture arrangements, property options, authorities, construction contracts, sales contracts, consultants' agreements, finance agreements, and many other items associated with property development.

As you become more knowledgeable and experienced you will require less legal advice and be able to refine the aspects of advice that you actually need.

For site acquisition you may wish to obtain town planning and conveyance advice.

For any proposed joint venture or property option agreement you may also wish to obtain property advice.

Where authorities are concerned there are a myriad of potential legal services that you may require. Investigate which ones are appropriate before you travel this path.

Sales agreements and conveyance for the end product that you are selling may also require property advice. Similarly, if you are leasing the end product a property lawyer may be necessary.

Your design and other consultants will need to be engaged with appropriate contracts; construction lawyers may be required for this.

You may need legal advice from a construction lawyer when it comes to your building contract.

Finance agreements may require input from a commercial lawyer also.

I'm not trying to scare you with all this, I'm simply trying to make you aware of your risk management requirements. Everything comes down to risk. Protecting yourself legally is always a good idea.

Learning: Engaging lawyers early in your project will help you to establish your project with appropriate risk management put in place.

Insurance

There are always "what if" scenarios that play out in my mind when working on property development projects. There are so many different scenarios that can happen, its mind boggling, but you can't let these get in your way.

You must simply plan, prepare and monitor an appropriate risk management strategy for your project.

Insurance is risk management. It takes care of a number of risk issues for you and is readily affordable and can easily be costed for your feasibility analysis.

Depending on which country, state or territory, or locality you are proposing to develop within, the laws are all different. I believe that the general types of insurance remain the same. Always obtain advice from an insurance expert before you undertake a project.

Public and products liability insurance is a must for property owners. This insurance protects you against claims from members of the public.

Professional indemnity insurance is a must for consultants. This insurance protects the consultant against claims from their clients for negligence relating to their design work or advice. As a client I would insist on my consultants having this insurance as an error could be very costly and it is likely that the consultants would not have adequate financial resources to meet the costs of rectification.

Workers compensation insurance (or equivalent; check with your insurance broker) is a must for any employer. This insurance covers employees of companies against loss of wages/salary from work related injuries. Whenever a company is undertaking any work for me I insist on them having this insurance in place to protect me from claims made by that company's employees against me.

Construction risk insurance is critical for any construction project that is undertaken. This insurance covers the cost of rebuilding the then constructed works if it is damaged during the construction period. I will not commence any project without this insurance.

All these insurance policies have various peculiarities and I recommend that you speak to an insurance broker or insurance lawyer to obtain relevant advice regarding which insurances are appropriate for you and your proposed project in your relevant jurisdiction as terminology and requirements may vary.

Learning: Insurance is simply risk management. Insurance mitigates risk for a cost.

Procurement

When you need something and you get it that is called procurement.

Similarly, when you need help to undertake any part of your proposed development you will need to procure experts to provide you with the relevant product or service you require. These can be suppliers, builders, design consultants, lawyers; virtually anyone that provides a service or product.

Throughout the course of a property development project you are likely to require many varied services. You will need to procure these.

Procurement in a simplistic form is simply buying something. When you undertake a property development project you will need to buy things, whether they are services of consultants or goods from suppliers to install into the project. It is all procurement.

To be able to procure something you must know exactly what it is that you want to buy. In the case of services this can be a little daunting as you must clearly describe the services that you require the consultant to provide and when you need them.

When you are talking about design there are many different consultants that you will require to work together to complete your project design. Each different type of consultant will need to understand what your expectations are.

Your expectations are described by using a document called a "scope of works". This document identifies exactly what you expect from your services supplier.

When you request service providers to quote, this is called tendering. Tendering requires the service provider to provide a quotation to deliver the services that you have requested in accordance with your tender documents.

Tender documents are the entire set of documents that you provide the service provider in order for them to be able to tender. The tender documents will include the scope of works and other relevant documents.

Other relevant documents to include in your tender could be the proposed contract that you will require the consultant to execute if they are successful, copies of current drawings or similar information, details of the proposed site, a schedule (or program) for delivery of the services, a description of the proposed development and anything else that will assist the service provider understand your requirements.

Ordinarily I would obtain three quotations for each service that I required on a project. This would ensure that I am receiving value for money and would enable me to review the tenders to examine whether I had missed anything in the scope of works (some service providers are very good at clearly defining the services they propose to provide, which can assist you greatly).

Upon receipt of the tenders I always compare them to ensure that I have an "apples for apples" comparison. Just because one price is lower than another does not mean that the lower price is cheaper than the other. Sometimes tenders can exclude particular items that you want included or allow for a greater scope of works than you thought you required; or simply they can be at cross purposes with your requirements.

It is essential that you properly compare all tenders that you receive and prepare comparative tables. Document the content of the tenders in detail to ensure that you do not miss anything that is relevant.

Once you have your preferred tenderer you may need to negotiate with them before executing a contract or agreement.

If you procure appropriately, plan your time wisely, and clearly articulate your requirements, you are more likely to achieve a good result.

Learning: Being clear about exactly what you require and the contract terms and conditions will assist you to achieve appropriate tenders (based upon your nominated risk profile) within a reasonable timeframe.

Consultants

Service providers are consultants. Consultants generally "sell" expertise or advice.

Some consultants will be required on your property development project to provide expert advice whilst others will provide design.

Lawyers provide advice, architects provide design; both are consultants and service providers.

A builder or contractor, although a service provider, is not a consultant as they provide goods and services. This is the best way that I can describe the difference for you.

Consultants will provide you with everything you need to make your project happen, except for the actual building and construction works.

So what types of consultants are there and what services might they provide for you?

Let's look at things progressively for your project. Firstly you are likely to require a town planner to assist with the legislative framework surrounding property development and the town plan.

Next you might require the services of a quantity surveyor to provide indicative construction costs for your proposed form of construction.

Perhaps you will require the services of a land surveyor to survey the proposed site to properly identify it and to provide information for the design consultants.

You are going to require a number of different design consultants to prepare documents for the authority approvals and for the building and construction tender. These consultants may include an architect, structural engineer, civil engineer, hydraulic engineer, mechanical engineer, fire engineer and a building code surveyor.

Check these requirements with your experts or with your local authority.

Each consultant provides a particular sector of expertise that could be essential to the successful design of your proposed project.

Possibly the single most important consultant that you may require is the property development consultant. I say this not simply because this is what I do, but I say this as property development consultants are experts in managing the property development process.

Also note that I did say "may require" as you could well be able to undertake numerous activities yourself. However I do suggest that if you undertake a project by yourself and you are a beginner, at an absolute minimum have a property development consultant available in that capacity. They will advise you on when other experts are required.

All property developers have someone fulfil the role of development manager. In large property development companies these persons are usually employees.

Consultants will always need to be properly managed. Make sure you administer their contracts appropriately and provide clear directions.

Learning: All consultants are experts in their fields. Use their expertise instead of guessing. It will be a lot cheaper in the long run than making mistakes that result in loss of time and loss of profit.

Design

Your design consultants will create your design initially for your authority approval and then for construction.

But before we go too far we need to discuss how to undertake the design process.

Every form of property development is different however the process is fundamentally the same.

When you first commence a project you will need a sketch design. This will be a rough, hand drawn "scrawl" created by the architect in conjunction with the information provided by the town planner.

Don't forget that your sketch design will be driven by your due diligence into the market you are intending to develop your end product for. Your due diligence would have told you what the market needs and what it is willing to pay for it.

The sketch design will give you, the client, some parameters with which to instruct your design consultants on how to proceed.

At this time I would engage a quantity surveyor to provide high level cost advice on the sketch design. This will tell you whether the sketch design is within your construction budget for your project.

Following the sketch design your design consultants will create a concept design. The concept design is a little more detailed than the sketch design and will start to take on some genuine shape and form with input from a number of consultants, not just the architect.

Again I would have the quantity surveyor give you some cost advice at this stage; always checking the cost against the budget.

The next stage of the design process is the authority approvals stage. Here the design is further developed to a stage where the interior layout of the building, clearly identifying the proposed use, is prepared and the external façade is identified. The height, bulk and scale of your building/s are clearly determined and, usually, artists' impressions of the finished building are created.

Before making an application to the authority, I would again have the quantity surveyor check the construction cost against the budget.

After the authority application stage you need to complete your design. This is what we call full documentation.

Each design consultant must fully and completely design the entirety of the project always seeking to avoid errors, omissions and ambiguities.

Equally important is the coordination of the design to ensure that each of the design consultant's designs "works" when overlaid with the other design consultant's designs. For example, inside a ceiling there is limited space, you need to make sure that air conditioning ducts can pass and that there are no structural beams or hydraulic pipes in the way.

Now you have a fully designed building. Again I would have the quantity surveyor do a cost check against your budget however with one difference; the cost check must be undertaken progressively during the full design stage. What you don't want is a cost problem after the design is complete.

Learning: Construction is usually the largest single cost in your feasibility. If your design lacks buildability or is expensive it may detrimentally impact on your feasibility. Get your design right.

Cost control

Knowing where you money is going is critical to your success on a property development project.

Within your feasibility you have identified all the potential cost areas for your project and, of course, your revenue. In my experience you should focus your attention on the larger numbers first and then the smaller ones.

What this means is that the number one priority on your project has to be your revenue. This must be the largest number in your feasibility otherwise you don't make a profit.

If you lose revenue you can get into a lot of trouble! Keep your eye on this!

Depending on what type of project you are doing, the next largest cost is likely to be your construction cost. Within the design chapter I have mentioned to you that having a quantity surveyor doing cost checking as your building design progresses is a good way of ensuring that you meet your construction budget.

However in my experience it doesn't matter how good your quantity surveyor is, when you tender the building and construction works the tenders you receive may differ substantially from what your quantity surveyor said.

This is not an indictment on the quantity surveyor; the market will always advise you what the price is at the time that the work is tendered.

After the construction cost there could be a myriad of different costs competing for your attention. My suggestion here is simply to allocate priority to the larger numbers, but this doesn't mean that you ignore the others as a lot of small losses add up to a large number very quickly.

To keep your costs controlled you will need to make sure that your contracts with all your service providers are administered properly and that the scope of services required is clearly identified and understood.

Always update your feasibility cashflow every single month; this will be your financial lifeline.

Learning: Focus on the largest numbers first but don't lose sight of the smaller numbers. Keep accurate cost records so that you can see if things are heading in the wrong direction early. You need to take action when you see a problem.

Authorities

Wherever you are planning on developing your project there will be authorities involved.

For example you are likely to have an approval authority such as local government (possibly regional and national depending on what your proposal is), a road authority, an airport authority, water and sewer authority, a telecommunications authority and an energy supply authority (potentially two if you think electricity and gas).

Your proposal may require approvals from some or all of these or other authorities.

When considering your project make sure you undertake due diligence on which authorities have jurisdiction over your proposed site and for your proposed project.

When you know which authorities are involved you can properly plan for their requirements during the relevant design stage and include appropriate cost allowances if applicable.

Some authorities are easy to deal with whilst others are a challenge. What you need to do is make things as easy as possible for the authorities to assess your application and approve it, or at least ask you questions as quickly as possible so that you can resolve any matter they raise promptly.

As always, time is money and in my experience authorities do not operate with these constraints in mind. Most authorities have a charter to provide responses within certain time parameters and they do their best to achieve these. But making things easy for them helps immensely.

The people that work within the authorities are no different to anyone else, they are there to undertake a role and to work certain hours for their pay. Nobody wants to have a difficult time at work and when applications come along that are easy to assess people appreciate this.

I have heard a lot of people complain about authorities taking too long to approve applications however with my projects I rarely have this situation occur. I prepare good quality applications and regularly speak with the person within the authority to provide any assistance necessary.

Treat everyone in an authority as you would like to be treated.

Learning: Provide professionally prepared complete documentation to make the relevant authority's job easy.

Building contractors

All your planning, preparation and design comes under scrutiny when construction commences.

Traditionally, builders have very tight margins and low tolerance for client caused delays. The most common form of building contract, the lump sum (also known as fixed price and hard dollar) is adversarial in nature.

The builders who tendered are in a competitive situation vying for a contract of a large nature. All your tenderers will want to win the project given their efforts required to provide a tender.

In this situation where competition is fierce and margins are narrow, the successful tenderer is likely to look for every opportunity to improve their profit margin.

This is where it becomes essential that all of your project documents are correct; no errors, no omissions, no ambiguities, everything 100% correct.

We all make mistakes. There will be some in your project documents and you are likely to have to compensate the builder for rectifying these, but that is why you have a contingency.

If the mistakes cost a lot of money you can always consider seeking recompense from whoever caused the problem in the first place; legal advice is required before you start anything of this nature.

Remember that your building contractor is your friend; they are creating the product that you intend to make your profit from; keep them building in a timely manner.

In the next chapter, Superintendence of Building Works, I will discuss how to manage your building contract.

Learning: Your building contractor is your friend. You need them to deliver your project on time, on budget, and with the agreed quality standard.

Superintendence of building works

Your builder has a contract and certain obligations to meet, make sure that they do.

Don't forget that you have obligations too and that you must meet yours also.

You may have heard the old adage that you should sign the contract and put it in the bottom drawer. To me this is the worst possible thing you could do!

Contracts require you and the building contractor to do certain things at certain times. How would you know what these were if you put the contract in the bottom drawer?

In my experience it is essential that you have an independent person acting as the superintendent of your building contract.

The superintendent role is to manage the client's obligations under the building contract. In different types of contracts or in different locations this role may be called the Principal's Representative, the Project Manager, Clerk of Works or another term. In each case the intent is the superintendence of the building contract.

Some common actions the superintendent takes is to monitor the progress of construction, to monitor the quality of the progressing works, to assess progress claims, to assess claims for variations and extensions of time, to act in response to notices of dispute, to issue payment certificates, to create defects lists and to undertake all these things within the timeframes required within the building contract.

The building contractor has similar obligations to make its claims within certain timeframes and various parameters defined within the building contract.

In some building contracts the superintendent must act as an independent party and in others the superintendent is an agent of the principal. Most builders are likely to prefer the superintendent being an independent party.

Superintendence of the building contractor is essential to ensure you end up with the end product that you require on the date you require it.

Learning: The superintendent will ensure that your project is delivered in accordance with the terms and conditions of the contract that you sign with the building contractor. Make sure that the contract has your required time, cost and quality standards clearly identified.

Sales and marketing

Whatever the product is that you are creating, you must achieve your revenues for it. That means you either have to sell it or lease it.

Throughout this book we have used an example of a medium density housing property development project, so let's continue with this example.

Very early on you must decide what you need as inclusions in your project so that you can include these in your sales and marketing collateral.

What are the key features of your development that you will utilise to obtain enquiry? How will you attract people to your project instead of the competition? These are interesting questions and another of those critical success factors for you.

Remember that to de-risk a project you need to sell as much of the property as you can before you start construction. Your financier is likely to require you to do this also, to at least cover the value of the expected debt.

Once construction starts you are seriously committed to the project.

"What if" remains the biggest issue for you to consider at this time. What if they don't sell and you have finished building?

As part of your due diligence you would have researched the market in your proposed area to determine that there was a demand. This research would also have told you what the market needs and at what price.

So you already know what is required, all you need now is to convert this into the design of your project and into your marketing collateral.

You will need to engage the services of an experienced off-the-plan sales agent if you don't intend to sell the properties yourself. My preference would be to use an experienced agent for this who has an established database to work from.

A database is a very valuable list of contact names and addresses that can be used to promote various properties to. These real estate agents spend years building their databases and utilise them to sell many projects. They are very valuable.

Armed with marketing collateral and an experienced off-the-plan real estate agent you are ready to launch your product to the market.

Pre-sales are a critical part of obtaining development finance so make sure that you sell as many properties as you can as quickly as possible to get your project started and de-risked.

Learning: Preparation of appropriate marketing collateral will dramatically improve your prospects of selling your product in a timely manner.

Settlements

Once your project nears completion you will need to prepare to receive your revenue.

Again assuming you are developing medium density housing you will have a number of properties that need to be settled.

Settlement means finalisation of the transaction for the sale of the property. Originally you sold the purchaser a proposed property which has now become an actual property. It's time to get paid for your property.

As the building work comes to completion you will need to obtain various certifications and, most critically, a certificate of title (or equivalent in your jurisdiction) for the newly created property. This is the key document that you need to complete your transaction.

Once armed with your certificate of title you can finalise the transaction and collect your revenue.

Your financier will probably require that you repay your debt first. No surprises here! Then all the revenue goes towards repaying your equity and finally, whatever is left is your profit.

The trick is to have some left over at the end of the day. Nobody likes undertaking a project for no reward or for a loss.

Learning: Prepare for settlement so that your revenue is received as early as possible.

Summary

If you have been considering undertaking a property development and have read this book you will have been exposed to some information for you to contemplate.

You can make a lot of money when you acquire your site by either buying at a very good price or by delaying the settlement date on that transaction; or both!

Your profit in a property development is about de-risking the project.

Risk comes in all types of forms and you must consider them all. I have given you many to consider however there are many more.

Seek expert advice prior to and throughout the duration of your project. This expert advice is essential to a successful outcome on your project however please keep in mind that not all property development projects end up profitable, there are a myriad of things that can, and sometimes do, go wrong.

Whether you are proposing a residential, commercial, retail, industrial or some other form of development, do your research BEFORE you put any money into a proposed project.

Know your market.

Know the demand.

Know your price point.

Know what you are getting yourself into *before* you start.

I cannot stress enough the need for you to engage experts to assist you prepare your feasibility, to advise you on appropriate strategies throughout the course of the project and to guide you through all the processes and procedures that are required to undertake a property development.

One final comment; property development is business. It's not personal. Always participate in the process at a business level.

I wish you every success with your property development. Feel free to update me on your property development experiences by sending an email to theadvantage@lefta.com.au.

About the Author

Steve Chandler is a third generation property developer, was born in Australia and raised in Australia and in Papua New Guinea.

From a young age Steve was exposed to construction and property development through both his father's and grandfather's work and businesses.

Steve commenced his career in the building industry in 1980. At the age of 21 Steve achieved his first managerial role in the building industry and quickly rose through the ranks to become a Project Manager. Following this Steve held Development Management roles with major property development companies.

In 2006 Steve established *LEFTA Corporation Pty Ltd*, a property development strategy, advisory and consultancy firm created to help people with their property development projects.

Steve commenced lecturing in construction project management and property development at various institutions in 2012.

Today Steve manages *LEFTA Corporation Pty Ltd* and has expanded its reach through provision of training, coaching and mentoring services including establishment of *Property Development Institute*, an online property development training institution designed to help you **BE** a property developer.

www.propertydevelopmentinstitute.com

Contact Steve at:

LEFTA Corporation Pty Ltd

PO Box 1699
Potts Point NSW 1335 Australia

Shop 5, The Village Centre
24-30 Springfield Avenue
Potts Point NSW 2011 Australia

P: +61 2 8004 6669

E: theadvantage@lefta.com.au
W: http://www.lefta.com.au

Made in the USA
Columbia, SC
26 October 2020